# ONE NATION,

# THROUGH *the eyes* OF A CHILD

PARENTING IN AMERICA
IN THE 21ST CENTURY

# ONE NATION,

# THROUGH *the eyes* OF A CHILD

THE **POPULAR** GROUP

This book was written by Walnut Grove Press for exclusive use by the Popular Publishing Company.

Popular Publishing Company LLC
1700 Broadway
New York, NY 10019

ISBN 1-59027-067-3

*The ideas expressed in this book are not, in all cases, exact quotations, as some have been edited for clarity and brevity. In all cases, the author has attempted to maintain the speaker's original intent. In some cases, material for this book was obtained from secondary sources, primarily print media. While every effort was made to ensure the accuracy of these sources, the accuracy cannot be guaranteed. For additions, deletions, corrections or clarifications in future editions of this text, please write Popular Publishing Company LLC.*

Certain elements of this text, including quotations, stories, and selected groupings of Bible verses, have appeared, in part or in whole, in publications produced by Walnut Grove Press of Nashville, TN; these excerpts are used with permission.

All scripture quotations, unless otherwise indicated, are taken from the HOLY BIBLE, NEW INTERNATIONAL VERSION ©. NIV ©. Copyright © 1973, 1978, 1984, by International Bible Society. Used by permission of Zondervan Publishing House. All rights reserved.

Scripture taken from the NEW AMERICAN STANDARD BIBLE®, Copyright © 1960, 1962, 1963, 1968, 1971, 1972, 1973, 1975, 1977, 1995 by The Lockman Foundation. Used by permission.

Scripture quotations marked (NKJV) are taken from The Holy Bible, New King James Version, Copyright © 1982 by Thomas Nelson, Inc. Used by permission.

Scripture quotations marked (NLT) are taken from The Holy Bible, New Living Translation, Copyright © 1996. Used by permission of Tyndale House Publishers, Incorporated, Wheaton, Illinois 60189. All rights reserved.

Printed in the United States of America
Page Layout Design by Bart Dawson
Cover Design: Tiffany Berry

1 2 3 4 5 6 7 8 9 10 • 02 03 04 05 06 07 08 09 10

# TABLE OF CONTENTS

—INTRODUCTION—

I T HAS NEVER BEEN EASY TO RAISE CHILDREN, BUT
today the challenges of parenting are of a
different nature and magnitude than those faced
by previous generations. Today, parents must guide
their children through minefields of 21st-century
temptations that have invaded the schoolyard, the
neighborhood, the television screen, and the family
computer. Add to this the uncertainty of a post-
September 11th world, and parents now face the
daunting task of raising responsible children in
difficult, uncertain, and sometimes frightening
times.

This book is intended to help. On the pages
that follow, a wide assortment of notable men and
women share words of wisdom and time-tested
methods of effective parenting. The text will
specifically address the concerns of American
families living in the long, dark shadow of
September 11th. How, we ask ourselves, can we
best help our children understand the events that
have reshaped our world? And, how can we best
encourage our families during a time when unseen
forces seem to threaten our very way of life? The
answers to these questions, and others like them,
can be found in the tried-and-true, common-sense

parenting tips on the pages that follow.

America remains a proud, strong, freedom-loving nation. But how does America appear to its children? It depends. The attitudes and beliefs of our children depend, in large part, upon us. If America is to remain strong and free, then we, as loving parents and grandparents, must do our part. The future of this nation is in our hands. Our kids are depending on us . . . and so is Uncle Sam.

# PART I

# ONE NATION:

*Through the Eyes of a Child*

# 1

## *What Our Children See*

I'D RATHER SEE A SERMON THAN
HEAR ONE ANY DAY; I'D RATHER
ONE SHOULD WALK WITH ME
THAN MERELY TELL THE WAY.

—

*Edgar A. Guest*

AMERICA IN THIS CENTURY CAN BE A DAUNTING place to raise children. We live in a world where our young people are exposed to an almost endless array of temptations, distractions, and decidedly mixed messages. Our children are often confronted with unhealthy peer pressures and unwelcome role models. But, despite the challenges of a difficult age, our kids will survive, and so will we.

In a world filled with disturbing images and inappropriate messages, we, as parents, must assume control over the content of the materials that our children view within the four walls of our own homes. And, we must prepare our young people for the images and the temptations that they will encounter in the world outside the home.

As parents, we must understand that *we* are our children's most important role models. For better or for worse, we are the men and women who provide living, breathing, up-close-and-personal examples for our children. The lessons that we *preach* are not nearly as important as the lessons that we *live*.

Unfortunately, lectures and sermons of the spoken variety have decidedly limited effectiveness unless they are accompanied by behaviors that reinforce those messages. The old strategy of "Do as I say, not as I do" simply does not work because our youngsters are far better observers than they are listeners. As parents, our best hope is to live our lives in accordance with the lessons we teach, and hope that our kids are watching (which, by the way, they are).

What do our children see? Sadly, they see too many images that are neither healthy nor appropriate. But, hopefully, our children also see parents who live responsibly and love whole-heartedly. In such cases, both children and parents are blessed.

HUMAN MODELS ARE MORE
VIVID AND MORE PERSUASIVE
THAN MORAL COMMENTS.

—

*Daniel J. Boorstin*

Our children do not follow our words but our actions.

*James Baldwin*

A person who lives right, and is right, has more power in his silence than another has by words.

*Phillips Brooks*

What you do speaks so loudly that I cannot hear what you say.

*Ralph Waldo Emerson*

Example is the school of humankind, and they will learn at no other.

*Edmund Burke*

The teaching process requires more than words; morality lessons, like all paternal preachments, are best taught by example.

*Mary Carlisle Beasley*


Setting an example is not the main means of influencing another, it is the only means.

*Albert Einstein*


In everything set them an example by doing what is good.

*Titus 2:7 NIV*


A good example is the best sermon.

*Thomas Fuller*

A child identifies his parents with God, whether adults want the role or not. Most children "see" God the way they perceive their earthly fathers and mothers.

*James Dobson*

We live. We die. The best we can do is to leave a worthwhile example for those who come after us.

*Adam Walinsky*

More depends upon my walk than upon my talk.

*D. L. Moody*

My father didn't tell me how to live; he lived, and let me watch him do it.

*Clarence Buddington Kellard*

YOU CANNOT NOT MODEL.
IT'S IMPOSSIBLE. PEOPLE WILL SEE
YOUR EXAMPLE, POSITIVE OR
NEGATIVE, AS A PATTERN FOR
THE WAY LIFE IS LIVED.

—

*Stephen Covey*

# —TIPS FOR PARENTS—

**TAKE CONTROL:** Monitor the images that your children view on television and on the Internet. You, as a responsible parent, must decide which messages and which images are appropriate for your child. The responsibility is yours and yours alone, not that of television executives or web page designers.

**MAKE YOUR ACTIONS CONSISTENT WITH YOUR WORDS:** Parental pronouncements are easy to make but much harder to live by. But whether you like it or not, you are almost certainly the most important role model for your child. Behave accordingly.

**DON'T BE AFRAID TO PREACH SERMONS . . . OCCASIONALLY:** Don't be afraid to talk with your child about your core beliefs, and never be afraid to discuss matters of personal safety or health. But, don't make your sermons too frequent or too condescending.

**WHEN YOU MAKE A MISTAKE, ADMIT IT:** No parent is perfect, not even you. Consequently, you will make mistakes from time to time (and yes, you might even lose your temper). When you make a mistake, apologize to the offended party, especially if that party is related to you by birth.

# 2

## *What Our Children Learn*

EDUCATION IS THE KEY TO UNLOCK
THE GOLDEN DOOR OF FREEDOM.

—

*Thomas Jefferson*

RESPONSIBLE PARENTS UNDERSTAND THE VALUE OF a good education. Children often do not. Therefore, we parents must assume responsibility for the education of our children during their formative years.

Gradually, our youngsters must assume control over the quality and effectiveness of their own educational experiences, but in the early years, that responsibility belongs to us, the parents. Teachers, of course, play an important role in the process, as do schools, but parents play the primary role.

Proper education begins with a thorough understanding of "the basics." The old familiar song praises the value of "readin' and writin' and 'rithmetic." And it still applies. Every child deserves an early exposure to the joys of reading, and every student deserves an education in the basic fundamentals of grammar and mathematics. When we allow our children to pass through the halls of academia without a firm grasp of "the fundamentals" of education, we do them a profound disservice—one with lifelong ramifications. But, when we prepare our youth with a firm foundation grounded in the basics of reading, writing, and mathematics, we prepare them for success, and we help provide for generations that are yet unborn.

A CHILD UNEDUCATED IS
A CHILD LOST.

—

*John F. Kennedy*

A child's education should begin at least a hundred years before he is born.

*Oliver Wendell Holmes, Sr.*

The only thing more expensive than education is ignorance.

*Ben Franklin*

At the desk where I sit, I have learned one great truth. The answer for all our national problems, the answer for all the problems of the world, is summarized in a single word. That word is "education."

*Lyndon Baines Johnson*

Genius without education is like silver in the mine.

*Ben Franklin*

Education is not
a preparation for life;
education is life itself.
—

*John Dewey*

I learned the importance of self-education. Once you realize that the learning is up to you, you have the right attitude to succeed in school and beyond.

*Tony Bennett*

You can get help from teachers, but you are going to have to learn a lot by yourself, sitting alone in a room.

*Dr. Seuss*

I think, at a child's birth, if a mother could ask a fairy godmother to endow it with the most useful gift, that gift would be curiosity.

*Eleanor Roosevelt*

The most important thing about education is appetite.

*Winston Churchill*

WE SHOULDN'T TEACH GREAT
BOOKS. WE SHOULD TEACH
A LOVE OF READING.

—

*B. F. Skinner*

Knowledge is power; knowledge is safety; knowledge is happiness.

*George Washington Carver*

The object of education is to prepare the young to educate themselves throughout their lives.

*Robert Maynard Hutchins*

Anyone who stops learning is old, whether at twenty or eighty.

*Henry Ford*

When I learn something new—and it happens every day—I feel a little more at home in this universe, a little more comfortable in the nest.

*Bill Moyers*

The truly human society is a learning society, where grandparents, parents, and children are students together.

*Eric Hoffer*

America's future will be determined by the home and the school. The child becomes largely what it is taught; hence, we must watch what we teach it and how we live before it.

*Jane Addams*

A man cannot leave a better legacy to the world than a well-educated family.

*Thomas Scott*

# —TIPS FOR PARENTS—

**READ TO YOUR CHILDREN:** Countless studies have clearly demonstrated the benefits of reading books to young children . . . read to yours every day.

**STRESS THE IMPORTANCE OF LEARNING:** Some families stress the importance of education more than other families. Make yours a home in which the importance of education is clearly a high priority.

**TEACH BY EXAMPLE:** Make continuing education an important part of your own life; your children will, in all likelihood, follow your example.

**DISCOVER ALTERNATIVE LEARNING TOOLS:** Today's world is chock-full of innovative teaching tools, especially those associated with computer-assisted learning. Invest in these tools and make certain that your children use them.

**MAKE LEARNING FUN:** Learning should never be confused with drudgery or with punishment. Your task, as a responsible parent, is to find ways to make the learning experience a pleasure for the child (including, of course, regular visits to the nearest zoo *and* the nearest children's museum).

# 3

# THE FUTURE:

THE FUTURE IS NOT OMINOUS,
BUT A PROMISE; IT SURROUNDS
THE PRESENT LIKE A HALO.

—

*John Dewey*

O N THE MORNING OF SEPTEMBER 11, 2001, THE future of America seemed uncertain at best. In fact, Americans of all ages struggled with the new reality of our times: danger in the homeland. But, the future of America is not nearly as dark as we might have feared on that terrible September day. And, we must share this message with our children: in America, the future remains a friend to those who prepare for it.

Ours is a generation populated with an overabundance of critics and skeptics. Bad news, it seems, can travel the globe before good news reaches the end of the street. Yet, we must not allow our young people to become skeptics, nor can we allow them to lose faith in the future. Maya Angelou correctly observed, "A cynical young person is almost the saddest sight to see, because it means that he or she has gone from knowing nothing to believing nothing." We must never allow our children to lose faith in the promise of tomorrow; we must, instead, train our youngsters to think optimistically about the possibilities that they will encounter in the years to come.

The American Dream is alive, well, and dwelling in the hearts of millions of young Americans; prayerfully, one of those young Americans is *yours*.

The good old days were never that good, believe me. The good new days are today, and better days are coming tomorrow. Our greatest songs are still unsung.

*Hubert H. Humphrey*

Anyone who fights for the future, lives in it today.

*Ayn Rand*

I am not afraid of tomorrow, for I have seen yesterday and I love today.

*William Allen White*

Never be afraid to trust an unknown future to a known God.

*Corrie ten Boom*

There will always be a frontier where there is an open mind and a willing hand.

*Charles Kettering*

Life is a preparation for the future; and the best preparation for the future is to live as if there were none.

*Elbert Hubbard*

The horizon leans forward, offering you space to place new steps of change.

*Maya Angelou*

Go forth and meet the shadowy future without fear.

*Henry Wadsworth Longfellow*

The future fairly startles me with its impending greatness. We are on the verge of undreamed progress.

*Henry Ford*

I don't like looking back. I'm looking ahead to the next show. It's how I keep young.

*Jack Benny*

If a man carefully examines his thoughts, he will be surprised to find how much he lives in the future. His well-being is always ahead.

*Ralph Waldo Emerson*

Now we must learn, from growth theory and self-actualization theory, that the future also now exists in the form of ideals, hopes, duties, tasks, plans, goals, unrealized potentials, mission, fate, and destiny.

*Abraham Maslow*

THIS FABULOUS COUNTRY,
THE PLACE WHERE MIRACLES NOT
ONLY HAPPEN, BUT WHERE THEY
HAPPEN ALL THE TIME.
—

*Thomas Wolfe*

METHUSELAH LIVED TO BE 969
YEARS OLD. YOU BOYS AND GIRLS
WILL SEE MORE IN THE NEXT FIFTY
YEARS THAN METHUSELAH SAW
IN HIS WHOLE LIFETIME.

—

*Mark Twain*

# —TIPS FOR PARENTS—

**FAMILIARIZE YOURSELF WITH THE OPPORTUNITIES OF TOMORROW:** The world of tomorrow is filled with opportunities for those who are willing to find them and work for them. Make certain that you have more than a passing familiarity with the ever shifting sands of our changing America. Then, share your insights with the young people who live under your roof.

**BE A BOOSTER, NOT A CYNIC:** Cynicism is contagious, and so is optimism. Think and act accordingly.

**FOCUS ON POSSIBILITIES, NOT ON STUMBLING BLOCKS:** Of course, you will encounter occasional disappointments, and, from time to time, you will encounter failure. So will your children. But, don't invest large quantities of your life focusing on past misfortunes. Instead, look to the future with optimism and hope . . . and encourage your children to do the same.

# 4

# "YES, I CAN":

## When Children Believe in Themselves

---

WHEN CHILDREN KNOW THEY
ARE VALUED, THEN THEY
FEEL VALUABLE.

—

M. Scott Peck

SADLY, WHEN MANY OF OUR CHILDREN GAZE INTO the mirror, they don't like what they see. Their dissatisfaction stems, in part, from their exposure to a near endless stream of images that glorify our nation's appetite for "perfect" role models. The media often sends messages to our children that are unhealthy, if not dangerous. These messages are both subtle and pervasive: our children are told that happiness is achieved by the rich, the famous, the thin, and the beautiful. And, to make matters worse, the standards by which our children are encouraged to judge themselves are, for the most part, impossible to achieve.

As responsible parents, we must continually remind our children that they are loved and that they are valuable *just as they are*, not as they might be if they were thinner, brighter, or more popular. We must help our children understand that the messages of the media are most certainly *not* meant to be guidelines for better living; those messages are, quite simply, means of generating profits for the companies that produce them. As caring parents, we must love our children without condition, and we must encourage our youngsters to extend that same kind of love *to themselves*.

What sorts of images do our children see when they turn on the television or go to the movies?

Images of perfection. But, when the screen goes black, all of us, children and adults alike, must return to the real world, not one that is created in Hollywood or on Madison Avenue. May we teach our children that in *this* world, they need not be perfect to be loved.

TO FIND LIFE REASONABLY
SATISFYING, YOU MUST HAVE
A SELF-IMAGE YOU CAN LIVE WITH.

—

*Maxwell Maltz*

Respect children because they're human beings and they deserve respect. If you do, they'll grow up to be better people, and they'll respect themselves.

*Benjamin Spock*

The person who does not value himself cannot value anything or anyone.

*Ayn Rand*

The worst loneliness is not to be comfortable with yourself.

*Mark Twain*

Once you learn to validate your own existence, you have the wind in your sails—then the only question is: where do you want to go?

*Carlos Santana*

If you can't stand yourself, neither can anybody else.

*Sid Caesar*

A person cannot be comfortable without his own approval.

*Mark Twain*

The privilege of a lifetime is being who you are.

*Joseph Campbell*

He who is able to love himself is able to love others also.

*Paul Tillich*

If you make friends with yourself you will never be alone.

*Maxwell Maltz*

Everybody must learn this lesson somewhere—it costs something to be what you are.

*Shirley Abbot*

A happy life is one which is in accordance with its own nature.

*Seneca*

Look for the good in everybody, starting with yourself.

*Marie T. Freeman*

THE ULTIMATE LESSON ALL OF US
HAVE TO LEARN IS UNCONDITIONAL
LOVE, WHICH INCLUDES NOT ONLY
OTHERS BUT OURSELVES AS WELL.

—

*Elizabeth Kübler-Ross*

# —TIPS FOR PARENTS—

**EXPOSE THE MYTHS:** From time to time, sit down and talk with your children about the images that they see and the expectations they hold for themselves. Remind your youngsters that the Hollywood dream factory is not the real world.

**VALIDATE YOUR CHILDREN:** In your own eyes, your children are perfect, or nearly so. Make certain that you communicate your love, your admiration, and your devotion many times each day.

**VALIDATE YOURSELF:** You, too, may be caught up in the modern-day push toward perfection, and if you are, your attitude will be contagious. When you "lighten up" on yourself, you will, in turn, do the same for your children.

# PART II

# LESSONS FROM THE HOME FRONT:

*What Parents Teach*

5

*Love*

THE ABILITY TO LOVE IS THE HEART
OF THE MATTER. THAT IS HOW WE
MUST MEASURE OUR SUCCESS OR
FAILURE AT BEING PARENTS.

—

*Gloria Vanderbilt*

THE BEAUTIFUL WORDS FROM THE NEW TESTAMENT remind us of a profound truth: "But now abide faith, hope, love, these three; but the greatest of these is love" (1st Corinthians 13: 13 NASB). And so it is with parenting. Of all the tools in our parental toolkit, the greatest by far is love.

Even the most well-informed parent can make mistakes, and so will you. But love has the power to overcome those mistakes. And, even the most well-mannered child will, on occasion, misbehave, and so will yours. But with love and time, immature behavior can be corrected.

Do you seek to give your child a gift that cannot be taken away? Look within your heart and share the love that you find there. No gift is greater; no gift is more important; no gift is more enduring.

THE SECRET OF A HAPPY HOME LIFE
IS THAT THE MEMBERS OF THE
FAMILY LEARN TO GIVE AND
RECEIVE LOVE.
—

*Billy Graham*

No human creature could receive or contain so vast a flood of love as I often felt after the birth of my child.

*Dorothy Day*

Children who are truly loved, although in moments of pique they may consciously feel or proclaim that they are being neglected, unconsciously know themselves to be valued. This knowledge is worth more than gold.

M. *Scott Peck*

The love we give away is the only love we keep.

*Elbert Hubbard*

Children are the hands by which we take hold of heaven.

*Henry Ward Beecher*


Love stretches your heart and makes you big inside.

*Margaret Walker*


Where there is great love there are always miracles.

*Willa Cather*


Love is the essence of God.

*Ralph Waldo Emerson*

Nobody has ever measured, not even poets, how much the heart can hold.

*Zelda Fitzgerald*

The story of a love is not important—what is important is that one is capable of love. It is perhaps the only glimpse we are permitted of eternity.

*Helen Hayes*

If one wishes to know love, one must live love.

*Leo Buscaglia*

Genuine love is volitional rather than emotional. The person who truly loves does so because of a decision to love.

M. Scott Peck

CHILDREN NEED LOVE,
ESPECIALLY WHEN
THEY DO NOT DESERVE IT.

—

*Harold S. Hulbert*

Before you were conceived, I wanted you. Before you were born, I loved you. Before you were here and home, I would die for you. This is the miracle of love.

*Maurene Hawkins*

If a thing loves, it is infinite.

*William Blake*

Love seeks one thing only: the good of the one loved. It leaves all the other secondary effects to take care of themselves. Love, therefore, is its own reward.

*Thomas Merton*

Love is the healer, the reconciler, the inspirer, the creator . . . .

*Rosemary Haughton*

LOVE WINS WHEN
EVERYTHING ELSE WILL FAIL.

—

*Fanny Jackson Coppin*

# —TIPS FOR PARENTS—

**EXPRESS YOURSELF:** Your children need to hear that you love them . . . from you! If you're bashful, shy, or naturally uncommunicative, get over it.

**BE CREATIVE:** There are many ways to say, "I love you." Find them. Put love notes in lunch pails and on pillows; hug relentlessly; laugh and play with abandon.

**BE CONSISTENT:** Of course, there will be times when you feel anger toward your children, but your love for them should never be in question. Parental love must never be turned on and off like the garden hose; it should, instead, flow like a mighty river, too deep to touch bottom and too strong to stop.

# 6

## *Time with Our Children*

# ONE TODAY IS WORTH
# TWO TOMORROWS.

—

*Ben Franklin*

I F LOVE IS THE FIRST TOOL IN THE PARENTS' TOOLKIT, time is the second. Our children need our love, of course, but they also need our presence. Yet, we live in a society that is filled to the brim with distractions, and we may find it harder and harder to spend sizable amounts of time with our children. No matter. As responsible parents, we must *make* the time to spend with our youngsters; nothing is more important.

In recent years, a distinction has arisen between "quality time" and "quantity time." Let us not delude ourselves: our children need both. And, for that matter, so do we. Stephen Covey writes, "Creating a warm, caring, supportive, encouraging environment is probably the most important thing you can do for your family." Creating that environment takes time. When you make the time for family time, you reap enduring rewards for yourself *and* for your kids.

I DON'T BUY THE CLICHÉ THAT
QUALITY TIME IS THE MOST
IMPORTANT THING. IF YOU
DON'T HAVE ENOUGH QUANTITY,
YOU WON'T GET QUALITY.

—

*Leighton Ford*

Time is the coin of your life. It is the only coin you have, and only you can determine how it will be spent. Be careful lest you let other people spend it for you.

*Carl Sandburg*

There is so much to teach, and the time goes so fast.

*Erma Bombeck*

To those who would say, "We don't have time to do these things!" I would say, "You don't have time not to!"

*Stephen Covey*

The best use of life is to spend it for something that outlasts life.

*William James*

Time is so precious that God deals it out only second by second.

*Fulton J. Sheen*

When we love something it is of value to us, and when something is of value to us, we spend time with it, time enjoying it and time taking care of it. So it is when we love children: we spend time admiring them and taking care of them. We give them our time.

*M. Scott Peck*

"SUZANNE WILL NOT BE AT SCHOOL TODAY," I ONCE WROTE TO HER TEACHER. "SHE STAYED AT HOME TO PLAY WITH HER MOTHER." I DON'T REMEMBER MANY OTHER DAYS OF HER ELEMENTARY YEARS. BUT, I REMEMBER THAT DAY.

—

*Gloria Gaither*

We must use time creatively, and forever realize that the time is always ripe to do right.

*Nelson Mandela*

If we only knew the real value of a day.

*Joseph Farrell*

May you live all the days of your life.

*Jonathan Swift*

When the family is together, the soul is at peace.

*Russian Proverb*

# —TIPS FOR PARENTS—

**MINIMIZE DISTRACTIONS:** There is an important difference between spending time with your children and simply occupying space with them; recognize the difference and take appropriate action. For starters, turn off the television set. Then, take whatever steps are necessary to capture the attention of your children. Today's world is full of distractions for kids and adults alike. Minimize them.

**MAKE AN APPOINTMENT WITH YOUR CHILD . . . AND KEEP IT:** If you find it difficult to find enough time for your child, put him or her on your daily calendar and then keep the appointment.

**GET AWAY FROM THE DAILY ROUTINE:** One surefire way to capture time with your child is to pack up the family car and leave home for a day or two. And, while you are in the car, why not turn off the radio?

# 7

## *Listening to Our Children*

# THE FIRST DUTY OF LOVE
# IS TO LISTEN.

—

*Paul Tillich*

N O PARENT CAN BE A PERFECT LISTENER. OUR children simply talk too much, and the distractions of work and home life are simply too great for parents to measure carefully every word. But, on occasion, parents must become *very* careful listeners. During times of uncertainty and fear, when the television screen is filled with violence and destruction, parents must do the improbable; they must turn off the television, sit down face-to-face, and enter into two-way conversations with their kids.

Listening is a skill that improves with practice. But, as parents, most of us are more practiced in the art of lecturing than we are in the art of listening. Lecturing our children, of course, is the easier of the two skills to master. When we lecture, the podium is ours, and we can recite the same litany of advice that was recited to us when *we* were children. Unfortunately, most youngsters suffer from a common malady: parent deafness. In other words, when the lecture begins, the listening ends. Yet it need not be so.

If we want our children to hear our words, then we, in turn, must hear theirs. And, when we listen, we learn. If asked, our children will—in most cases—tell us what's on their minds. We learn about their concerns, their fears, and their peers. We hear about their hopes, their dreams, and their plans. And then, because we have taken time to hear *their* concerns, our children become more likely to hear *ours*…and everybody wins.

# HEARING IS ONE OF THE BODY'S FIVE SENSES, BUT LISTENING IS AN ART.

—

*Frank Tyger*

To listen is an effort, and just to hear is no merit. A duck also hears.

*Igor Stravinsky*

The art of conversation lies in listening.

*Malcolm Forbes*

He who listens well learns well. Listening is the single most important on-the-job skill that a good leader can cultivate.

*Bill Marriott*

The reason that we have two ears and only one mouth is that we may listen the more and talk the less.

*Zeno of Citium*

I think the one lesson I have learned is that there is no substitute for paying attention.

*Diane Sawyer*

All wise men share one trait in common: the ability to listen.

*Frank Tyger*

Listening is a commitment and a compliment. It is a commitment to understand how the other person feels, and it is a compliment because it says, "I care about what's happening to you."

*Matthew McKay*

Listen with sincerity.

*Joe Girard*

A prudent question is one-half of wisdom.

*Francis Bacon*

It is better to know some of the questions than to know all of the answers.

*James Thurber*

To be able to ask a question clearly is two-thirds of the way to getting it answered.

*John Ruskin*

Be a good listener. Your ears will never get you in trouble.

*Frank Tyger*

THERE IS ONLY ONE RULE
FOR BEING A GOOD TALKER:
LEARN HOW TO LISTEN.

—

*Christopher Morley*

# —TIPS FOR PARENTS—

LISTEN FIRST, THEN SPEAK: For most parents, the temptation to lecture is great. It takes conscious effort to hold one's tongue until one's ears are fully engaged. When a parent is able to do so, his or her efforts are usually rewarded.

IF AT FIRST YOU DON'T SUCCEED, KEEP LISTENING: If your child is uncommunicative, don't give up; continue to listen and keep responding with love and encouragement; in all likelihood, the communication between the two of you will eventually improve.

MAKE CONVERSATIONS AS PLEASURABLE AS POSSIBLE: Every parent knows that sometimes a stern lecture is in order. But, every serious conversation between a parent and child should not be an occasion for the gnashing of teeth; parents should engage their children in positive, uplifting, encouraging conversations whenever possible; otherwise, children simply "tune out" their parents.

# 8

## *Communicating with Children*

IT'S NOT WHAT YOU TELL THEM;
IT'S WHAT THEY HEAR.

—

*Red Auerbach*

EVEN IF YOU HAPPEN TO BE THE WORLD'S GREATEST listener, there will come a time, and soon, when your child will need a good, old-fashioned talking-to. But how can you best get your message across? That question, of course, has puzzled parents of every generation, and our generation is no different. But, when all else fails, we can call upon the following time-tested rules for high-quality communications:

1. How you say what you say is often as important as what you say.

2. When angry, count to ten; if still angry, keep counting.

3. Keep your message as simple as possible, if not simpler.

4. When you wish to communicate an important message, have a goal in mind. When you have achieved your goal, stop.

5. If you are uncertain whether or not your message is getting through, pause and ask questions.

6. And finally, remember the words of Franklin D. Roosevelt, "Be sincere. Be brief. Be seated."

Now, having read these helpful hints, and being motivated by the sincere desire to communicate with your children, you are free to begin talking . . . slowly.

A VOCABULARY OF TRUTH AND
SIMPLICITY WILL BE OF SERVICE
THROUGHOUT LIFE.

—

*Winston Churchill*

When parents have time for their kids, when they get together almost every day for conversation and interaction, then their teens do much better in school and life.

*James Dobson*

How you say it might be as important as what you say.

*Harvey Mackay*

You can communicate without motivating, but it impossible to motivate without communicating.

*John Thompson*

The most valuable of all talents is that of never using two words when one will do.

*Thomas Jefferson*

A speaker is never successful till he has learned to make his words smaller than his ideas.

*Ralph Waldo Emerson*

Part of good communication is listening with the eyes as well as with the ears.

*Josh McDowell*

Parents need to make a concerted effort to build bridges to their kids, starting very early to have fun as a family, laughing and talking and doing things that bond the generations together.

*James Dobson*

A spoonful of humor makes the message go down easier.

*Frank Leahy*

Something that has really helped me communicate with my kids is to ask their opinions.

*Josh McDowell*

See things from the other person's point of view and talk in terms of his wants and needs.

*Frank Bettger*

People don't care how much you know until they know how much you care about them.

*Zig Ziglar*

Too often we underestimate the power of a touch, a smile, a kind word, a listening ear, an honest compliment, or the smallest act of caring, all of which have the potential to turn a life around.

*Leo Buscaglia*

All the fun is how you say a thing.

*Robert Frost*

Put your information across slowly and repeat it over and over again! Take a difficult point and make it so simple that it will become clear to everyone.

*Knute Rockne*

Short words are best and old words when short are best of all.

*Winston Churchill*

Don't throw away your friendship with your teenager over behavior that has no great moral significance. There will be plenty of real issues that require you to stand like a rock. Save your big guns for those crucial confrontations.

*James Dobson*

Reasoning with a child is fine, if you can reach the child's reason without destroying your own.

*John Mason Brown*

The real menace in dealing with a five-year-old is that in no time at all you begin to sound like a five-year-old.

*Jean Kerr*

# CHILDREN HAVE MORE NEED
# OF MODELS THAN CRITICS.

—

*Joseph Joubert*

# —TIPS FOR PARENTS—

**PLAN AND PREPARE:** When you have an important topic to discuss, plan your conversation in advance; have an idea of the topics you wish to discuss; have clear goals for your discussion.

**CONTROL THE SETTING:** Choose a relatively quiet setting and minimize distractions wherever possible (translation: turn off the television); the family automobile can be a good, non-threatening place to engage in conversation *if* the radio remains in its "off" position.

**ASK OPEN-ENDED QUESTIONS:** When questions can be answered with a simple "yes" or "no," youngsters will tend to answer accordingly; a better strategy is to ask questions that require a more thoughtful response. Such questions might begin with: "How do you feel about…" or "What do you think about…."

# 9

## *Encouraging Our Children*

MY MOTHER TOLD ME I WAS
BLESSED, AND I HAVE ALWAYS
TAKEN HER WORD FOR IT.

—

*Duke Ellington*

ALL OF US, INCLUDING OUR CHILDREN, NEED AN occasional pat on the back. But children, being the sensitive souls that they are, may need more pats than the rest of us. So it is up to us, as parents, to provide our kids with a heaping helping of back-patting.

Plato advised, "Be kind, for everyone you meet is fighting a hard battle." And sometimes, our children fight battles against discouragement and doubt that leave them fearful and anxious. We parents are the reserve troops who help our children survive and conquer the inevitable skirmishes of their lives.

As parents, the words we speak to our children have great power. How wise is the parent who can measure his or her words carefully. But sometimes, in the rush to have our messages heard, we speak first and think later…with unfortunate results.

If you seek to be the most encouraging parent you can possibly be, measure your words carefully. Speak wisely, not impulsively. When you do, your words will offer encouragement and hope to a family—and to a world—that needs both.

A YOUNG PERSON SHOULD NEVER
BE MADE TO FEEL THAT NO GREAT
THING IS EXPECTED OF HIM OR HER.

—

*Father Flanagan*

PARENTS SHOULD ALWAYS WATCH
FOR OPPORTUNITIES TO OFFER
GENUINE, WELL-DESERVED PRAISE
TO THEIR CHILDREN, WHILE
AVOIDING EMPTY FLATTERY.

—

*James Dobson*

Never tell a young person that anything cannot be done. God may have been waiting centuries for someone ignorant enough of the impossible to do that very thing.

*John Andrew Holmes*

It's a father's job to convince his children that they are gifted. Ultimately, it's the child's job to use that gift.

*J. R. Freeman*

Never miss an opportunity to say a word of congratulations.

*Lyndon Baines Johnson*

For every one of us who succeeds, it's because there's somebody there to show us the way.

*Oprah Winfrey*

How many people stop because so few say, "Go!"
*Chuck Swindoll*

You cannot teach a child to take care of himself unless you will let him try. He will make mistakes; and out of these mistakes will come his wisdom.
*Henry Ward Beecher*

Invest in the human soul. Who knows, it might be a diamond in the rough.
*Mary McLeod Bethune*

A lot of people have gone further than they thought they could because someone else thought they could.

*Zig Ziglar*

# ENCOURAGEMENT IS THE OXYGEN OF THE SOUL.

—

*John Maxwell*

Children are not so different from kites. Children were created to fly. But they need wind, the undergirding and strength that come from unconditional love, encouragement, and prayer.

*Gigi Graham Tchividjian*

Discouraged people don't need critics. They hurt enough already. They don't need more guilt or piled-on distress. They need encouragement. They need a refuge, a willing, caring, available someone.

*Chuck Swindoll*

Let us consider how to stimulate one another to love and good deeds.

*Hebrews 10:24 NASB*

Perhaps once in a hundred years a person may be ruined by excessive praise. But surely once every minute someone dies inside for the lack of it.

*Cecil G. Osborne*

Everybody wants to be somebody. The thing you have to do is give them the confidence that they can become the kind of people they want to become.

*George Foreman*

Great people are those who make others feel that they, too, can become great.

*Mark Twain*

Each child is an adventure into a better life— an opportunity to change the old pattern and make it new.

*Hubert H. Humphrey*

In the final analysis it is not what you do for your children, but what you have taught them to do for themselves, that will make them successful human beings.

*Ann Landers*

Treat people as if they were what they should be, and you help them become what they are capable of becoming.

*Goethe*

MY FATHER GAVE ME
THE GREATEST GIFT ANYONE
COULD GIVE ANOTHER PERSON:
HE BELIEVED IN ME.

—

*Jim Valvano*

# —TIPS FOR PARENTS—

**MAKE YOURSELF A SOURCE OF ENCOURAGEMENT TO EVERYONE, NOT JUST YOUR CHILDREN:** To become practiced in the art of encouragement, you need practice.

**NEVER CONFUSE ENCOURAGEMENT WITH PITY:** Pity parties are best left unattended by you *and* by your children.

**NEVER CONFUSE ENCOURAGEMENT WITH IDLE FLATTERY:** Kids are smart; they can distinguish between the two.

**MAKE ENCOURAGEMENT A HABIT:** Deliberately look for ways to encourage and praise your children . . . every day. Good deeds and good words can become habit-forming.

**DON'T FRET OVER FAILURES:** Encourage your children for their efforts even if those efforts don't achieve the desired results. Winning isn't everything.

# 10

## *Discipline*

LIFE IS TONS OF DISCIPLINE.

—

*Robert Frost*

A S PARENTS, WE HAVE A RESPONSIBILITY TO OUR children to teach them that discipline is not a four-letter word. To the contrary, children who lead disciplined, orderly lives are, by and large, happier than those who live under the cloud of unfinished work and unfulfilled promises.

Unfortunately, we live in a society where too many role models live lives characterized by irresponsibility and excess. Our job, as parents, is to lead disciplined lives ourselves and to teach our children to do the same.

Parents know all too well that even in a wealthy nation like America, life holds few rewards for the undisciplined. But, for those who are willing to engage in shoulder-to-the-wheel hard work, America is still a land of boundless opportunities. Therefore, wise parents teach discipline by word and by example, but not necessarily in that order.

# LOVE, WITHOUT DISCIPLINE, ISN'T.

—

*Malcolm Forbes*

We are incapable of teaching our children self-discipline unless we ourselves are self-disciplined.

M. *Scott Peck*

You cannot be disciplined in great things and undisciplined in small things.

*George S. Patton*

In reading the lives of great men, I found that the first victory they won was over themselves: with all of them, self-discipline came first.

*Harry S Truman*

# SELF-COMMAND IS
# THE MAIN DISCIPLINE.

—

*Ralph Waldo Emerson*

Father was the old-fashioned sort who believed that the authority in the home belonged to parents and not to the children.

*Vance Havner*

When properly applied, loving discipline works! It stimulates tender affection, made possible by mutual respect between parent and a child. It bridges the gap that otherwise separates family members who should love and trust each other.

*James Dobson*

The alternative to discipline is disaster.

*Vance Havner*

The goal of disciplining our children is to encourage their growth as respectful, responsible, self-disciplined individuals.

*Don H. Highlander*

LOVING A CHILD DOESN'T MEAN
GIVING IN TO ALL HIS WHIMS;
TO LOVE HIM IS TO BRING OUT
THE BEST IN HIM, TO TEACH HIM
TO LOVE WHAT IS DIFFICULT.

—

*Nadia Boulanger*

No horse gets anywhere
until he is harnessed.
No stream or gas drives
anything until it is confined.
No Niagara is ever turned
into light and power
until it is tunneled.
No life ever grows great
until it is focused,
dedicated, disciplined.

—

*Henry Emerson Fosdick*

# THE MOST POWERFUL PERSON IS HE WHO HAS HIMSELF IN HIS OWN POWER.

—

*Seneca*

# —TIPS FOR PARENTS—

**BE DISCIPLINED IN YOUR OWN APPROACH TO LIFE:** You can't teach it if you won't live it.

**AS CHILDREN GROW OLDER, GIVE THEM AGE-APPROPRIATE RESPONSIBILITIES:** Household chores can be wonderful teaching tools. Employ them.

**EXPECT SOME CHAOS, BUT NOT TOTAL CHAOS:** Of course, children are messy and disorganized, but there should be limits to everything, including your kids' disorganization; set those limits and enforce them.

**FOLLOW THROUGH ON YOUR OWN COMMITMENTS AND INSIST THAT YOUR CHILDREN DO LIKEWISE:** When you make a promise, keep it. When your children make a commitment, see that they do the same.

# 11

## *Teaching Integrity*

# THE INTEGRITY OF THE UPRIGHT
# SHALL GUIDE THEM....

—

*Proverbs 11:3 KJV*

Helen Keller could have been speaking about this generation when she observed, "Character cannot be developed in ease and quiet. Only through trial and suffering is the soul strengthened." At the turn of the new millennium, we live in a character-building time.

Character is built slowly over a lifetime. It is the sum of every right decision, every honest word, every noble thought, and every heartfelt prayer. It is forged on the anvil of honorable work and polished by the twin virtues of generosity and humility. Character is a precious thing—difficult to build but easy to tear down. As Americans who value honor and truth, we must seek to live each day with discipline, integrity, and faith. When we do, integrity becomes a habit. And God smiles upon us and upon our nation.

As responsible parents, we must teach integrity by our words and, more importantly, by our deeds. None other than the father of our country, George Washington, wrote, "The most enviable of all titles: an honest man." Mr. Washington's observation reminds us that character counts. It did in his day; it does now; it always will.

IN MATTERS OF STYLE,
SWIM WITH THE CURRENT;
IN MATTERS OF PRINCIPLE,
STAND LIKE A ROCK.

—

*Thomas Jefferson*

Children miss nothing in sizing up their parents. If you are only half-convinced of your beliefs, they will quickly discern that fact.

*James Dobson*

Be careful with truth towards children; to a child, the parent or teacher is the representative of justice.

*Margaret Fuller*

Maintaining your integrity in a world of sham is no small accomplishment.

*Wayne Oates*

WE ARE EFFECTIVE ONLY WHEN
WE HAVE INTEGRITY,
WHEN OUR ACTIONS ARE IN LINE
WITH OUR VALUES.

—

*Stephen Covey*

Integrity is the glue that holds our way of life together. We must constantly strive to keep our integrity intact. When wealth is lost, nothing is lost; when health is lost, something is lost; when character is lost, all is lost.

*Billy Graham*

Honesty is the first chapter in the book of wisdom.

*Thomas Jefferson*

Virtue is its own reward.

*John Dryden*

RECOMMEND VIRTUE TO YOUR
CHILDREN; THAT ALONE—NOT
WEALTH—CAN GIVE HAPPINESS.

—

*Ludwig van Beethoven*

The most exhausting thing in life is being insincere.

*Anne Morrow Lindbergh*

Truth is the only safe ground to stand upon.

*Elizabeth Cady Stanton*

Character is higher than intellect.

*Ralph Waldo Emerson*

Character building begins in infancy and ends in death.

*Eleanor Roosevelt*

No amount of ability is of the slightest avail without honor.

*Andrew Carnegie*

Happiness is not the end of life; character is.

*Henry Ward Beecher*

For when the one Great Scorer comes to write against your name, He marks not that you won or lost, but how you played the game.

*Grantland Rice*

# —TIPS FOR PARENTS—

**DISPLAY INTEGRITY IN MATTERS BOTH GREAT AND SMALL:** Right is right and wrong is wrong whether the issue appears large or inconsequential. And when it comes to issues of integrity, you are a 24-hour-a-day example to your child, so be on guard.

**DISCUSS THE IMPORTANCE OF INTEGRITY:** Teach the importance of integrity every day, and, if necessary, use words.

**IF YOUR CHILD TELLS A FALSEHOOD, TALK ABOUT IT:** Even "little white lies" are worthy of a parent-to-child talk; the bigger the lie, the bigger the talk.

# 12

## Lessons About Courtesy and Kindness

GRACEFULNESS HAS BEEN DEFINED
TO BE THE OUTWARD EXPRESSION
OF THE INWARD HARMONY
OF THE SOUL.

—

William Hazlitt

THE TWIN VIRTUES OF COURTESY AND KINDNESS never go out of style. And, if our children are to learn the rules of common courtesy and common decency, we, as responsible parents, must teach them.

Philosopher and naturalist Henry David Thoreau observed, "Goodness is the only investment that never fails." And, the noted American theologian Phillips Brooks advised, "Be such a person, and live such a life, that if every person were such as you, and every life a life like yours, this earth would be God's Paradise." One tangible way to make the world a more godly place is to spread kindness and courtesy wherever we go.

Children of all ages are tempted to engage in hurtful, uncivilized behavior. We must train them to do otherwise. May we, as parents, teach our children that courteous behavior is not only a surefire way to make the world a better place, but that it is also a surefire way to make *them* better people.

Ill customs and bad advice are seldom forgotten.

*Ben Franklin*

Rudeness is the weak man's imitation of strength.

*Eric Hoffer*

Say and do what you mean, but never say and do it meanly.

*Harvey Mackay*

Manners require time, as nothing is more vulgar than haste.

*Ralph Waldo Emerson*

Good manners are made up of petty sacrifices.

*Ralph Waldo Emerson*


Small kindnesses, small courtesies, small considerations, habitually practiced in our social intercourse, give a greater charm to the character than the display of great talents and accomplishments.

*Mary Ann Kelty*


Politeness is an inexpensive way of making friends.

*William Feather*

GOOD MANNERS ARE
THE TECHNIQUES OF EXPRESSING
CONSIDERATION FOR
THE FEELINGS OF OTHERS.

—

*Alice Duer Miller*

And as ye would that men should do to you, do ye also to them likewise.

*Luke 6:31 KJV*

Be enthusiastic. Every occasion is an opportunity to do good.

*Russell Conwell*

Seek to do good, and you will find that happiness will run after you.

*James Freeman Clarke*

KINDNESS IS THE UNIVERSAL
LANGUAGE THAT ALL PEOPLE
UNDERSTAND.

—

*Jake Gaither*

Do good to your friends to keep them, to your enemies to win them.

*Ben Franklin*

The older you get, the more you realize that kindness is synonymous with happiness.

*Lionel Barrymore*

In life, you can never do a kindness too soon because you never know how soon it will be too late.

*Ralph Waldo Emerson*

Never mistake kindness for weakness.

*Red Skelton*

Lead the life that will make you kindly and friendly to everyone about you, and you will be surprised what a happy life you will live.

*Charles Schwab*

Love is not just some great abstract idea or feeling. There are some people with such a lofty conception of love that they never succeed in expressing it in the simple kindnesses of ordinary life.

*Paul Tournier*

You have not lived a perfect day, even though you have earned your money, unless you have done something for someone who will never be able to repay you.

*Ruth Smeltzer*

The best portion of a good man's life is his little, nameless, unremembered acts of kindness and of love.

*William Wordsworth*

And be ye kind one to another, tenderhearted, forgiving one another.

*Ephesians 4:32 KJV*

When you extend hospitality to others, you're not trying to impress people; you're trying to reflect God to them.

*Max Lucado*

He climbs the highest who helps another up.

*Zig Ziglar*

I must admit that I personally measure success in terms of the contributions an individual makes to her or his fellow human beings.

*Margaret Mead*

We must not slacken our efforts to do good to all, especially to those with needs that will not be met if we fail in our common task of service to humanity.

*Danny Thomas*

The highest test of the civilization of any race is in its willingness to extend a helping hand to the less fortunate. A race, like an individual, lifts itself up by lifting others up.

*Booker T. Washington*

There is a very real relationship, both quantitatively and qualitatively, between what you contribute and what you get out of this world.

*Oscar Hammerstein II*

# —TIPS FOR PARENTS—

**COURTESY AND GOOD MANNERS START AT HOME:** If your children don't learn mannerly behavior at the family dinner table, they won't learn it anywhere else.

**YOU ARE AN EXAMPLE; BE A GOOD ONE:** Your children will learn how to treat others by watching you; be courteous to everyone, starting with those who live under your roof.

**LANGUAGE 101:** Unfortunately, your children will grow up in a profanity-laced world. Help them understand that they will be judged by the words they speak, and help them to choose those words with care.

**RESPECT FOR ALL PEOPLE:** Children may seek to find humor in the misfortunes of others; children may, on occasion, exhibit cruelty towards other children. Be watchful for such behaviors and correct them with enthusiasm and vigor.

# 13

## Parenting with Patience

ALL GOOD ABIDES WITH HIM
WHO WAITS WISELY.

—

Henry David Thoreau

Parenting requires patience—LOTS OF patience. And yet, a casual visit to the local shopping mall yields countless examples of impatient, undisciplined parents and their temper-tantrum-throwing kids. As we watch mothers and fathers pass by with their youngsters in tow, we all too often see tempers flare, tantrums start, yelling, yanking, pleading, foot-stomping, pouting, arguing, and tears. And, the children behave almost as badly!

When we, as parents, lose control of our emotions, we invite our youngsters to do likewise. That is why we, being the adults in the family, must exercise extreme patience as we love and care for our families.

From time to time, even the most mannerly children may do things that worry us, or confuse us, or anger us. Why? Because they are children and because they are human. And, it is precisely because they are human that we must, from time to time, be patient with our children's shortcomings (just as they, too, must be patient with ours). Patience is not only the price we pay for being responsible parents; it is also a lesson that we *must* teach our children . . . by example.

Genius is nothing more than a greater aptitude for patience.

*Ben Franklin*

There is no great achievement that is not the result of patient working and waiting.

*Josiah Gilbert Holland*

Adopt the pace of nature; her secret is patience.

*Ralph Waldo Emerson*

PATIENCE AND DILIGENCE,
LIKE FAITH, MOVE MOUNTAINS.

—

*William Penn*

Never do anything when you are in a fit of temper, for you will do everything wrong.

*Baltasar Gracián*

Anger is never without a reason, but seldom a good one.

*Ben Franklin*

Mistrust anger.

*Ben Hecht*

Speak when you're angry, and you'll make the best speech you'll ever regret.

*Laurence Peter*

KEEP COOL;
ANGER IS NOT AN ARGUMENT.

—

*Daniel Webster*

WHENEVER YOU ARE ANGRY,
BE ASSURED THAT IT IS NOT ONLY
A PRESENT EVIL, BUT ALSO THAT
YOU HAVE INCREASED A HABIT.

—

*Epictetus*

Consider how much more you often suffer from your anger and grief, than from those very things for which you are angry and grieved.

*Marcus Antonius*

Anger dwells only in the bosom of fools.

*Albert Einstein*

No person can think clearly with his fists clenched.

*George Jean Nathan*

He that can have patience can have what he will.

*Ben Franklin*

A man watches his pear tree day after day, impatient for the ripening of the fruit. Let him attempt to force the ripening fruit, and he may spoil both fruit and tree. But let him patiently wait, and the ripe pear, at length, falls into his lap.

*Abraham Lincoln*

Patience is the companion of wisdom.

*St. Augustine*

TAKE NO ACTION IN A FURIOUS
PASSION. IT'S PUTTING TO SEA
IN A STORM.

—

*Thomas Fuller*

EXPECT TROUBLE AS
AN INEVITABLE PART OF LIFE AND
REPEAT TO YOURSELF THE MOST
COMFORTING WORDS OF ALL:
THIS, TOO, SHALL PASS.

—

*Ann Landers*

# —TIPS FOR PARENTS—

**TAKE SEVERAL DEEP BREATHS AND COUNT TO FIFTY:** Counting to ten won't be nearly enough.

**TALK; DON'T STEW:** If a problem is bothering you, don't stew over it; talk about it with the appropriate person. Conversations can prevent conflagrations.

**GET LOTS OF REST:** If you're fuse is chronically short, perhaps you're simply tired. Try this experiment: turn off the television at 8:00 and put your family and yourself to bed. Besides, there is probably nothing on television worth watching anyway.

**LOOK FOR THE HUMOR:** As comedians know all too well, tragedy and comedy are traveling companions. If you become angry over one of the minor inconveniences of life, don't take your problem or yourself too seriously. Instead, look for a good reason to laugh; chances are, you'll find it.

# 14

## *Lessons in Faith*

FAITH OUGHT NOT TO BE
A PLAYTHING. IF WE BELIEVE,
WE SHOULD BELIEVE LIKE GIANTS.

—

Mary McLeod Bethune

AMERICA REMAINS A LAND OF PROSPERITY AND opportunity, but it is also a land that faces an uncertain future. In the years to come, our children will undoubtedly face challenges that we can scarcely fathom today. For that reason, we must arm our youth with an indispensable tool that will carry them through good times and bad. That tool is faith: faith in themselves, faith in their nation, faith in their collective future, and faith in an ultimate power beyond their own.

When the sun is shining and all is well, we find it easy to be optimistic about the world in which we live. But, when life takes an unexpected turn for the worse, as it does from time to time, our faith is tested to the limit. It is during these darker days of life that our children will need to draw upon all of their inner resources.

As parents, we are wise to prepare our children for the inevitable struggles of life. By stressing the importance of optimism and faith, we give to the next generation a priceless gift that they, in turn, can pass on to *their* children.

May God bless America *and* the young people whom He has entrusted to our care.

IF FEAR IS CULTIVATED,
IT WILL BECOME STRONGER;
IF FAITH IS CULTIVATED IT WILL
ACHIEVE MASTERY.

—

*John Paul Jones*

I never really look for things. I accept whatever God throws my way. Whichever way God turns my feet, I go.

*Pearl Bailey*

The whole course of things goes to teach us faith. We need only obey. There is guidance for each of us, and by lowly listening we shall hear the right word.

*Ralph Waldo Emerson*

FAITH IS ONE OF THE FORCES BY
WHICH MEN LIVE, AND THE TOTAL
ABSENCE OF IT MEANS COLLAPSE.

—

*William James*

Never take away hope from any human being.

*Oliver Wendell Holmes, Sr.*

Trust in God. Even if you fail Him, He will never fail you.

*Marie T. Freeman*

Faith can put a candle in the darkest night.

*Margaret Sangster*

FAITH CAN GIVE US COURAGE
TO FACE THE UNCERTAINTIES
OF THE FUTURE.

—

*Martin Luther King, Jr.*

Faith and doubt are both needed, not as antagonists, but working side by side to take us around the unknown curve.

*Lillian Smith*

This, then, is the state of the union: free and restless, growing, and full of hope. So it was in the beginning. So it shall always be, while God is willing, and we are strong enough to keep the faith.

*Lyndon Baines Johnson*

There are no hopeless situations; there are only people who have grown hopeless.

*Clare Boothe Luce*

Do not build up obstacles in your imagination. Difficulties must be studied and dealt with, but they must not be magnified by fear.

*Norman Vincent Peale*

I am an optimist. It does not seem to be much use being anything else.

*Winston Churchill*

On the human chessboard, all moves are possible.

*Miriam Schiff*

Faith is a spiritual spotlight that illuminates the path.

*Helen Keller*

We must accept finite disappointment, but we must never lose infinite hope.

*Martin Luther King, Jr.*

Perpetual optimism is a force multiplier.

*Colin Powell*

The essence of optimism is that it takes no account of the present, but it is a source of inspiration, of vitality, and of hope where others have resigned. It enables a man to hold his head high, to claim the future for himself, and not to abandon it to his enemy.

*Dietrich Bonhoeffer*

The only limit to our realization of tomorrow will be our doubts of today. Let us move forward with strong and active faith.

*Franklin D. Roosevelt*

THE SUN SHINES NOT ON US,
BUT IN US.

—

*John Muir*

*And in Conclusion . . .*

SAM LEVENSON JOKED, "INSANITY IS HEREDITARY, you can get it from your kids." Moms and dads understand what he meant. And an anonymous parent once observed, "A loving family is a thing of beauty and a *job* forever." Unfortunately, this statement is only partially true. Parenting is, of course, a job, but the work of raising our children is not "forever"; it is temporary. Still, we can be comforted in the knowledge that *the fruits* of our parental labors, our children (and their children), outlive us just as surely as our children influence the world in ways that we can never fully comprehend.

The philosopher George Santayana wrote, "A family is a masterpiece of nature." May you, as a devoted parent, help create the kind of living, breathing masterpiece that is a tribute to its creator . . . and to yours.